Th

Journaling your dreams, is showing God that you are a good steward over the prophecy he is speaking to you. Habakkuk was commissioned by God to write the vision he received. Habakkuk 2:2 states:

And the LORD answered me, and said, Write the vision, and make it plain upon tables, that he may run that readeth it. For the vision is yet for an appointed time, but at the end it shall speak, and not lie: though it tarry, wait for it; because it will surely come, it will not tarry.

Keeping God's visions before you will remind you of your purpose and destiny. Journaling you dream will help you unlock understanding and revelation. It' is my prayer that your spiritual eyes be open and that you are flooded with new possibilities for your future.

Proverbs 25:2

It is the glory of God to conceal a matter, but the glory of kings is to search out a matter.

I had a dream about:

My feelings about the dream:

_____

_____

_____

_____

_____

_____

_____

_____

_____

_____

_____

_____

_____

_____

_____

_____

_____

_____

_____

I had a dream about:

My feelings about the dream:

_____

_____

_____

_____

_____

_____

_____

_____

_____

_____

_____

_____

_____

_____

_____

_____

_____

_____

I had a dream about:

My feelings about the dream:

_____

_____

_____

_____

_____

_____

_____

_____

_____

_____

_____

_____

_____

_____

_____

_____

_____

_____

_____

_____

Ezekiel 11:24-25

And the Spirit lifted me up and brought me in a vision by the Spirit of God to the exiles in Chaldea So the vision that I had seen left me. Then I told the exiles all the things that the LORD had shown me.

I had a dream about:

My feelings about the dream:

_____

_____

_____

_____

_____

_____

_____

_____

_____

_____

_____

_____

_____

_____

_____

_____

_____

_____

_____

_____

I had a dream about:

My feelings about the dream:

_____

_____

_____

_____

_____

_____

_____

_____

_____

_____

_____

_____

_____

_____

_____

_____

_____

_____

_____

_____

Genesis 46:2

God spoke to Israel in visions of the night and said, "Jacob, Jacob." And he said, "Here I am."

God spoke to Israel in visions of the night and said, "Jacob, Jacob." And he said, "Here I am."

I had a dream about:

My feelings about the dream:

_____

_____

_____

_____

_____

_____

_____

_____

_____

_____

_____

_____

_____

_____

_____

_____

_____

_____

_____

I had a dream about:

My feelings about the dream:

_____

_____

_____

_____

_____

_____

_____

_____

_____

_____

_____

_____

_____

_____

_____

_____

_____

_____

_____

Daniel 2:28

"However, there is a God in heaven who reveals mysteries, and He has made known to King Nebuchadnezzar what will take place in the latter days. This was your dream and the visions in your mind while on your bed.

I had a dream about: _____

_____

_____

_____

_____

_____

_____

_____

_____

_____

_____

_____

_____

_____

_____

_____

_____

_____

_____

_____

My feelings about the dream:

_____

_____

_____

_____

_____

_____

_____

_____

_____

_____

_____

_____

_____

_____

_____

_____

_____

_____

_____

_____

_____

I had a dream about:

My feelings about the dream:
_____
_____
_____
_____
_____
_____
_____
_____
_____
_____
_____
_____
_____
_____
_____
_____
_____
_____
_____
_____
_____
_____

I had a dream about: _____

My feelings about the dream:

_____

_____

_____

_____

_____

_____

_____

_____

_____

_____

_____

_____

_____

_____

_____

_____

_____

_____

_____

_____

_____

I had a dream about:

Acts 16:9

A vision appeared to Paul in the night: a man of Macedonia was standing and appealing to him, and saying, "Come over to Macedonia and help us."

My feelings about the dream:

_____

_____

_____

_____

_____

_____

_____

_____

_____

_____

_____

_____

_____

_____

_____

_____

_____

_____

_____

_____

_____

Genesis 15:1

After these things the word of the LORD came to Abram in a vision, saying, "Do not fear, Abram, I am a shield to you; Your reward shall be very great."

I had a dream about: _____

_____

_____

_____

_____

_____

_____

_____

_____

_____

_____

_____

_____

_____

_____

_____

_____

_____

_____

_____

_____

_____

My feelings about the dream:

I had a dream about:

Exodus 3:2-3

The angel of the LORD appeared to him in a blazing fire from the midst of a bush; and he looked, and behold, the bush was burning with fire, yet the bush was not consumed. So Moses said, "I must turn aside now and see this marvelous sight, why the bush is not burned up."

My feelings about the dream:

_____

_____

_____

_____

_____

_____

_____

_____

_____

_____

_____

_____

_____

_____

_____

_____

_____

_____

_____

_____

_____

I had a dream about:

_____

_____

_____

_____

_____

_____

_____

_____

_____

_____

_____

_____

_____

_____

_____

_____

_____

_____

_____

_____

My feelings about the dream:

_____

_____

_____

_____

_____

_____

_____

_____

_____

_____

_____

_____

_____

_____

_____

_____

_____

_____

_____

_____

I had a dream about:

My feelings about the dream:

_____

_____

_____

_____

_____

_____

_____

_____

_____

_____

_____

_____

_____

_____

_____

_____

_____

_____

_____

_____

I had a dream about: _____

_____

_____

_____

_____

_____

_____

_____

_____

_____

_____

_____

_____

_____

_____

_____

_____

_____

_____

_____

_____

My feelings about the dream:
_____

_____

_____

_____

_____

_____

_____

_____

_____

_____

_____

_____

_____

_____

_____

_____

_____

_____

_____

Daniel 4:5

"I saw a dream and it made me fearful; and these fantasies as I lay on my bed and the visions in my mind kept alarming me.

I had a dream about:

My feelings about the dream:

I had a dream about:

My feelings about the dream:

_____

_____

_____

_____

_____

_____

_____

_____

_____

_____

_____

_____

_____

_____

_____

_____

_____

_____

_____

_____

_____

I had a dream about:

My feelings about the dream:

_____

_____

_____

_____

_____

_____

_____

_____

_____

_____

_____

_____

_____

_____

_____

_____

_____

_____

_____

_____

I had a dream about: _____

_____

_____

_____

_____

_____

_____

_____

_____

_____

_____

_____

_____

_____

_____

_____

_____

_____

_____

_____

My feelings about the dream:

_____

_____

_____

_____

_____

_____

_____

_____

_____

_____

_____

_____

_____

_____

_____

_____

_____

_____

_____

_____

I had a dream about: _____

_____

_____

_____

_____

_____

_____

_____

_____

_____

_____

_____

_____

_____

_____

_____

_____

_____

_____

Zechariah 3:1

Then he showed me
Joshua the high priest
standing before the angel
of the LORD, and Satan
standing at his right
hand to accuse him.

My feelings about the dream:

_____

_____

_____

_____

_____

_____

_____

_____

_____

_____

_____

_____

_____

_____

_____

_____

_____

_____

_____

I had a dream about: _____

_____

_____

_____

_____

_____

_____

_____

_____

_____

_____

_____

_____

_____

_____

_____

_____

_____

_____

_____

_____

_____

My feelings about the dream:

_____

_____

_____

_____

_____

_____

_____

_____

_____

_____

_____

_____

_____

_____

_____

_____

_____

_____

_____

_____

I had a dream about:

Acts 18:9

And the Lord said to Paul in the night by a vision, "Do not be afraid any longer, but go on speaking and do not be silent;

My feelings about the dream:

_____

_____

_____

_____

_____

_____

_____

_____

_____

_____

_____

_____

_____

_____

_____

_____

_____

_____

_____

_____

I had a dream about: _____

My feelings about the dream:

I had a dream about:

My feelings about the dream:

_____

_____

_____

_____

_____

_____

_____

_____

_____

_____

_____

_____

_____

_____

_____

_____

_____

_____

_____

_____

I had a dream about:

_____

_____

_____

_____

_____

_____

_____

_____

_____

_____

_____

_____

_____

_____

_____

_____

_____

_____

My feelings about the dream:

_____

_____

_____

_____

_____

_____

_____

_____

_____

_____

_____

_____

_____

_____

_____

_____

_____

_____

Revelation 1:12

Then I turned to see the
voice that was speaking
with me. And having
turned I saw seven golden
lampstands;

I had a dream about:

My feelings about the dream:

_____

_____

_____

_____

_____

_____

_____

_____

_____

_____

_____

_____

_____

_____

_____

_____

_____

_____

I had a dream about:

My feelings about the dream:

_____

_____

_____

_____

_____

_____

_____

_____

_____

_____

_____

_____

_____

_____

_____

_____

_____

I had a dream about:

Daniel 2:19

Then the mystery was revealed to Daniel in a night vision. Then Daniel blessed the God of heaven;

My feelings about the dream:

I had a dream about:

My feelings about the dream:

I had a dream about: _____

_____

_____

_____

_____

_____

_____

_____

_____

_____

_____

_____

_____

_____

_____

_____

_____

_____

_____

_____

My feelings about the dream:

I had a dream about: _____

My feelings about the dream:

Matthew 27:19

While he was sitting on the judgment seat, his wife sent him a message, saying, "Have nothing to do with that righteous Man; for last night I suffered greatly in a dream because of Him."

I had a dream about:

My feelings about the dream:

As you begin to journal your dreams and visions pray these scriptures daily. They will help you begin to see supernaturally and help with your understanding of dreams and visions.

Ephesians 1:18 I pray that the eyes of your heart may be enlightened, so that you will know what the hope of His calling is, what are the riches of the glory of His inheritance in the saints,

2 Kings 6:17 Then Elisha prayed and said, "O LORD, I pray, open his eyes that he may see." And the LORD opened the servant's eyes and he saw; and behold, the mountain was full of horses and chariots of fire all around Elisha.

James 1:5 But if any of you lacks wisdom, let him ask of God, who gives to all generously and without reproach, and it will be given to him.

JOURNALING TIPS

➤ Write down your dreams/visions or voice record them using a title and the date.

➤ Giving Honor to the revelation or prophetic word from God is the best way to bring increase into your life.

➤ The simple act of writing down your dreams will help you see the dream a different way and help to bring more understanding.

➢ Date your dream at the top of your page and note where you were at when you received it.

➢ Record your dream, including as much detail as you remember.

➢ Write out possible interpretations underneath the dream

➢ Try and interpret the major dream symbols, were they positive or negative?

➢ Write out questions about the dream. "Why was he shirt red?" "Why was my husband in that dream?"

We here at Rain Fire Ministries appreciate your dedication and support. We pray that you continue to pray, learn, and dive deeper into your spiritual walk with our Heavenly Father. Please visit our website rainfireministries.org for other helpful products and information about our ministry.

Made in the USA
Lexington, KY
27 July 2018